THE SONG OF YOU

THIRTY-DAY DEVOTIONAL

JAMES EDWARDS

This book is copyrighted by James Edwards. Copyright © 2018. All rights reserved.

ISBN-13: 978-1721181346

ISBN-10: 1721181342

No part of this publication may be reproduced, stored in a retrieval system or transmitted in any way by any means, electronic, mechanical, photocopy, recording, or otherwise, without the prior permission of the author except as provided by USA copyright law.

You can follow James on Facebook at his ministry page here: https://www.facebook.com/thewarriorscry or at his personal page here: https://www.facebook.com/awarriorscry

Cover designed by Jose Aljovin, http://www.josealjovin.com/

Edited by Lisa Thompson at www.writebylisa.com. You can email Lisa at writebylisa@gmail.com.

Scripture quotations marked "Phillips" are taken from The New Testament in Modern English, copyright 1958, 1959, 1960 J.B. Phillips and 1947, 1952, 1955, 1957. The Macmillian Company, New York. Used by permission. All rights reserved.

Verses marked CEB are taken from the Common English Bible® Copyright © 2010, 2011 by Common English Bible,™ Used by permission. All rights reserved worldwide, The "CEB" and "Common English Bible" trademarks are registered in the United States Patent and Trademark Office by Common English Bible. Use of either trademark requires the permission of Common English Bible.

Scripture quotations taken from the New American Standard Bible® (NASB), Copyright © 1960, 1962, 1963, 1968, 1971, 1972,

1973, 1975, 1977, 1995 by The Lockman Foundation. Used by permission. www.Lockman.org

Scripture quotations marked TPT are from The Passion Translation®. Copyright © 2017 by BroadStreet Publishing® Group, LLC. Used by permission. All rights reserved. www.thePassionTranslation.com.

Scripture quotations marked THE MIRROR: The Bible translated from the original text and paraphrased in contemporary speech with commentary. Copyright © 2014 by Francois du Toit. All rights reserved. Scripture taken from THE MIRROR. Copyright © 2014. Used by permission of The Author.

Scripture quotations marked NTE are from The New Testament for Everyone and are copyrighted © Nicholas Thomas Wright 2011.

Scripture quotations marked NLT are taken from the Holy Bible, New Living Translation, copyright ©1996, 2004, 2007, 2013, 2015 by Tyndale House Foundation. Used by permission of Tyndale House Publishers, Inc., Carol Stream, Illinois 60188. All rights reserved.

Scripture quotations marked MSG are taken from THE MESSAGE, copyright © 1993, 1994, 1995, 1996, 2000, 2001, 2002 by Eugene H. Peterson. Used by permission of NavPress. All rights reserved. Represented by Tyndale House Publishers, Inc.

Scripture quotations marked (KJV) are taken from the King James Version. Public Domain.

Scripture quotations marked (ESV) are from the ESV® Bible (The Holy Bible, English Standard Version®), copyright © 2001 by Crossway, a publishing ministry of Good News Publishers. Used by permission. All rights reserved.

Dedicated to my Mother, Kimberly Chandler Deese. She closed her eyes on Earth, November 15, 2017, and awoke to Jesus singing over her.

To my wife, Amber Edwards, for supporting me on this journey of seeing my first book to completion.

Special mention to Brian Edwards, my close friend who planted the seed for me to write a devotional!

INTRODUCTION

The Song of You is a beautiful lyric about how Father chose you to become his blameless child, adopted through the vicarious action of his Son, Jesus Christ, before the foundation of the Earth. You have been made holy, not just positionally, but fully holy. You have been made a vessel of his glory, fully reconciled to Father through Jesus, and reminded of this by Holy Spirit. This song is a lullaby sung over you while you cuddle up in his arms, a reassuring lilt during a time of struggle.

In this devotional, all the words are directed toward you, the reader, even though the truths in these pages are universal for anyone in Christ. Read these words over your own life. Read the scriptures

INTRODUCTION

in as many translations as you can get your hands on. In the upcoming thirty days, spend as much time in his presence as you can. By that, I mean to intentionally acknowledge his presence even though he is always with you.

1. JESUS IS WISDOM

> "Yet from this same God you have received your standing in Jesus Christ, and he has become for us the true wisdom, a matter, in practice, of being made righteous and holy, in fact, of being redeemed. And this makes us see the truth of scripture: 'He who glories, let him glory in the Lord.'"
>
> (1 Corinthians 1:31, Phillips)

Before we begin, remember that as a young child, you pursued wisdom as you grew older, often seeking the advice of a parent, grandparent, or various other mentors. These mentors taught you life lessons to help guide you in the way you should go, even sometimes disciplining you if you messed up. This is not unlike Father in heaven. If you lack wisdom, ask him, and he will grant it as James, the brother of Jesus, wrote in James 1:5. But what is wisdom?

According to James 3:17, wisdom that comes from above is pure and filled with peace, considerate and teachable, always filled with love and is never filled with judgment or hypocrisy. So when you receive the wisdom you seek, if it is accompanied by shame or condemnation, it is not Jesus. Remember the passage in 1 Corinthians 13 that details the love of God. Compare that passage with these verses in James.

Wisdom is Jesus is wisdom is love is Jesus. He is a full circle, and you can completely embrace your full reconciliation in him. Embrace Jesus in his wisdom; embrace wisdom in Christ.

2. JESUS IS GRACE

> "The grace of God has appeared, bringing salvation to all people. It educates us so that we can live sensible, ethical, and godly lives right now by rejecting ungodly lives and the desires of this world. At the same time, we wait for the blessed hope and the glorious appearance of our great God and savior Jesus Christ. He gave himself for us in order to rescue us from every kind of lawless behavior and cleanse a special people for himself who are eager to do good actions."
>
> (Titus 2:11–14, CEB)

Grace is often defined as "the unmerited favor of God." But even beyond unmerited favor, grace is the vicarious man. This man vicariously lived your life and died your death so that you can live completely through him while experiencing oneness with your Father in Jesus. Jesus is grace straight from our Father, and he came to become sin so that you would be grafted into the vineyard of grace. (See 2 Corinthians 5:21.) You were never meant to be excluded; you were always included.

Jesus, who was always in a constant relationship with Father, became the entrance for you into that same relationship. Your forehead now rests upon Father's forehead, his eyes looking deeply into your eyes as he whispers words of devotion and love over you.

You are the treasure in the field found by the man who ended up selling everything to obtain you. (See Matthew 13:44–46.) The man here is Jesus. He sold everything, gave up everything, and left his comfort and security for you. He longed for you so much that he left the ninety-nine to search for you and bring you home. (See Luke 15:3–4.) These are not the actions of a judge but the actions of a Father, longing to hold you close to his bosom once more.

So, yes, grace is the unmerited favor of God. But even more so, grace is the eternal Word of God spoken over you.

3. JESUS IS JUDGMENT

 "For God loved the world so much that he gave his only Son, so that everyone who believes in him shall not be lost, but should have eternal life. You must understand that God has not sent his Son into the world to pass sentence upon it, but to save it—through him. Any man who believes in him is not judged at all. It is the one who will not believe who stands already condemned, because he will not believe in the character of God's only Son. This is the judgment—that light has entered the world and men have preferred darkness to light because their deeds are evil. Anybody who does wrong hates the light and keeps away from it, for fear his deeds may be exposed. But anybody who is living by the truth will come to the light to make it plain that all he has done has been done through God."

(John 3:16–21, Phillips)

We have this idea that Father is the judge in the courtroom of life. We imagine him scorning at us from the bench. We also imagine that Jesus is our lawyer, and the devil is the prosecutor. In this courtroom, your life is played out: the devil accuses, Jesus defends, and Father ultimately judges you to eternal life or death. Furthermore, the Holy Spirit is nowhere to be found in this setting unless it's possibly as the court reporter, eagerly typing everything that plays out.

This imagery couldn't be any further from the truth. Father is a judge; that is true. But Jesus is not your lawyer, and the devil is not the prosecutor. That would be like the devil actually playing for the same team as Father, which is a laughable construct.

Take joy in this: Jesus is both the judgment of sin

and the verdict of your freedom in him. Jesus's mission was not to condemn, but to reconcile. He came to save, not to destroy. He came to reveal Father's heart for his creation. You are his creation, and you are seated in Christ Jesus *at* Father's right hand.

You have *already* been judged in Jesus; you have been judged the righteousness of God in Jesus (2 Corinthians 5:21).

4. JESUS IS OUR RIGHTEOUSNESS

 "He made Him who knew no sin to be sin on our behalf, so that we might become the righteousness of God in Him."

(2 Corinthians 5:21, NASB)

We are often reminded how filthy our righteousness is, how dirty those rags of flesh are that we dwell in. Sometimes when you mess up, you look in a mirror with anger at yourself, sickened about what you did. You know sin; you know it all too well, and you remind yourself every day when you do it. The good news is God the Son became your sin and substituted his righteousness for your sin. On the cross, he accepted you in him. You became his righteousness, and now you are seated in heavenly places at Father's right hand and in Jesus. (See Ephesians 2:6.)

I know what you are thinking because it's the same thing I thought when I first heard the message that I didn't have to sin because I am the righteousness of God in Jesus. You think, "That's impossible." But the good news is that it isn't. As 2 Corinthians 5:21 tells us, he became your sin so that you could become his righteousness. He became your flesh so that you could become his body. He became your filthy rags (Isaiah 64:6) so that you could become his pure and spotless Bride (Ephesians 5:25).

You are no longer filthy; your rags have been replaced with the most beautiful wedding dress you could imagine. You are no longer a sinner; you are the righteousness of God in Christ.

5. JESUS IS OUR RECONCILIATION

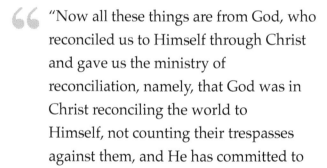 "Now all these things are from God, who reconciled us to Himself through Christ and gave us the ministry of reconciliation, namely, that God was in Christ reconciling the world to Himself, not counting their trespasses against them, and He has committed to us the word of reconciliation.

Therefore, we are ambassadors for Christ, as though God were making an appeal through us; we beg you on behalf of Christ, be reconciled to God."

(2 Corinthians 5:18–20, NASB)

This is a precursor to yesterday's verse and is found in the same book and chapter of 2 Corinthians. We see this last section of verse 20, and we hear "be reconciled to God." What does it mean to be reconciled to God? Is there an action involved? A work? How do you become reconciled to God?

Simple.

Jesus.

Father sent Jesus as an act of reconciliation for mankind to come back into communion with God, like we were in the Garden of Eden. You see, when Adam and Eve worked in the Garden, they worked without effort: no sweat or toil, no striving. They were in constant relationship with God, who walked with them in the Garden. It wasn't until Adam ate from the Tree of the Knowledge of Good and Evil that he worked by the sweat of his brow.

So you can see that in the Garden was just pure work: no exhaustion, no sweat, no strained muscles. They worked out of the abundant goodness of God.

Now you are fully and utterly reconciled to God so that whatever you do comes from your relationship with God and the abundance of Jesus, not your own efforts. Everything you accomplish, Jesus is running alongside of you to complete.

6. JESUS IS FORGIVENESS

> "As, therefore, God's picked representatives of the new humanity, purified and beloved of God himself, be merciful in action, kindly in heart, humble in mind. Accept life, and be most patient and tolerant with one another, always ready to forgive if you have a difference with anyone. Forgive as freely as the Lord has forgiven you. And, above everything else, be truly loving, for love is the golden chain of all the virtues."
>
> (Colossians 3:12–14, Phillips)

You are human. That's what you tell yourself every single time you fail. I know because that's what I used to tell myself. You look in the mirror, disgusted with yourself, mouthing hateful words or even saying them aloud. You have been taught from your childhood that your flesh is sin, and the actions of that flesh were sin. A few days ago, we talked about how we are constantly reminded that our own righteousness is filthy rags, but your righteousness now is Jesus. Take heart; not only is your righteousness Jesus, but so is your forgiveness.

Say it.

Go ahead.

Out loud.

"Jesus is my forgiveness."

Repeat it as many times as you need to hear it until it becomes a part of you. Write this truth upon your spirit, memorize it, and tattoo it on your heart.

"It is impossible for a good tree to produce bad fruit—as impossible as it is for a bad tree to produce good fruit. Do not men know what a tree is by its fruit? You cannot pick figs from briars, or gather a bunch of grapes from a blackberry bush! A good man produces good things from the good stored up in his heart, and a bad man produce evil things from his own stores of evil. For a man's words will always express what has been treasured in his heart" (Luke 6:43–45, Phillips).

Store it in your heart, and you will begin to see delicious fruit growing from your vine—not your fruit, but Jesus growing from you, and your actions reflecting the beautiful nature you have been given.

7. JESUS, OUR SHEPHERD

 "The Son of Man has come to give life to anyone who is lost. Think of it this way: If a man owns a hundred sheep and one lamb wanders away and is lost, won't he leave the ninety-nine grazing on the hillside and go out and thoroughly search for the one lost lamb? And if he finds his lost lamb, he rejoices over it, more than over the ninety-nine who are safe."

(Matthew 18:11–13, TPT)

We often hear Psalm 23 quoted.

"The Lord is my shepherd, I shall not want. He makes me lie down in green pastures; He leads me beside quiet waters. He restores my soul; He guides me in the paths of righteousness For His name's sake" (verses 1–3, NASB).

We identify Jesus as a shepherd, but we see this concept differently than Holy Spirit intends. In our minds, we rationalize his shepherding as a future event, as if Jesus isn't doing this constantly, thoroughly providing rest and sustenance for us.

The mob mentality here is that Jesus only interacts with you if you stay in the group. This couldn't be any further from the truth although we need to be plugged into fellowship with other believers. The truth is this: Jesus would leave the group in a heartbeat to go after the one, to ensure that the one isn't destroyed by the jaws of the bear or mauled by the lion. Matthew 18:12–14 tells us that he leaves the ninety-nine to look for the one. He has no desire to put you into turmoil and trouble or to lead you into evil snares. Rather his desire is for you to come home and *be* in him and him in you.

His desire is for you to graze in luscious green pastures next to the living water flowing from him into you. His desire is for you to just *be* in his rest, to take joy in his rest!

8. JESUS, OUR REDEEMER

> "Christ redeemed us from the curse of the Law by becoming a curse for us—because it is written, everyone who is hung on a tree is cursed. He redeemed us so that the blessing of Abraham would come to the Gentiles through Christ Jesus, and that we would receive the promise of the Spirit through faith."
>
> (Galatians 3:13–14, CEB)

In the beginning, you were deemed worthy because you were created in his image and likeness. Not only do you look like him, you *are* like him. He took *joy* in you before creation was even created. When he created Adam, he was thinking about you. When Adam ate from the Tree of the Knowledge of Good and Evil, Father cried out on account of you. He shouted through all the eons, "I did not create you for death!"

So he sent a part of himself, his Son, to become that death so that you could become part of his life. Your original design was that of relationship and bold communion with God. He deemed you worthy the moment he breathed breath into your lungs, but you fell away. Not because of anything you did but because creation fell with Adam.

Jesus came to redeem you and call you worthy because, in your mind, you were far from God even though he was singing over you since before you were formed in your mother's womb. (See Psalm 139.) You are his prize, and he takes joy in your joyfulness. He has set you as a seal upon his arm, as a seal upon his heart. (See Song of Songs 8:6.)

Take joy in this truth: you were deemed worthy and redeemed before Adam fell. You were found in Jesus eons before you were lost in Adam. God wasn't about to let you die. He rent heaven and earth on your behalf.

9. JESUS, OUR MIRROR

> "The days of window-shopping are over! In him every face is unveiled. In gazing with wonder at the blueprint of God displayed in human form, we suddenly realize that we are looking into a mirror, where every feature of his image articulated in Christ is reflected within us! The Spirit of the Lord engineers this radical transformation; we are led from an inferior mind-set to the revealed endorsement of our authentic identity."
>
> (2 Corinthians 3:18, The Mirror)

Almost all of us have been in a mirror maze at some point in our lives. You walk in and see your reflection on all the walls in front of you and behind you. You also see others who are trying to work their way through the maze. You hear the sounds of laughter throughout the halls as kids and adults run into mirrors and haphazardly find their way through.

You are the mirror maze for Jesus, and he is for you.

Let me explain. All things were created by him and through him. He *is* the Word and the words of God. His Word created you to be his playground, and he desires you to encounter the playground he created in himself for you. He takes joy in your happiness; he cries when you cry. He is sad when you are; he is angry when you are.

In your laughter, he laughs. When you are angry or hurt from the circumstances of life, he is too. He fully reflects you and you him. But as mirrors, we can sometime become broken, not by anything God has done, but by our own doing. When we don't love others, that scatters the love of God all over the place instead of powerfully focusing it at those around us. When we show hatred, disdain, or condemnation, we reflect nothing but the substance behind the mirror, not Jesus.

Remember, you are not just a human; you are radically different, a new creation, a divine creature seated in heavenly places in Jesus! (See Ephesians 2:6.) You are more than you ever imagined.

10. JESUS, OUR COMMUNION

 "As they ate, Jesus took the bread and blessed it and broke it and gave it to his disciples. He said to them, 'This is my body. Eat it.' Then taking the cup of wine and giving praises to the Father, he entered into covenant with them, saying, 'This is my blood. Each of you must drink it in fulfillment of the covenant. For this is the blood that seals the new covenant. It will be poured out for many for the complete forgiveness of sins. The next time we drink this, I will be with you and we will drink it together with a new understanding in the kingdom realm of my Father.'"

(Matthew 26:26–29, TPT)

With few exceptions, most churches only have communion once a month. They build it up and make it a pretty big deal, but then they do it, and it is over as quickly as it started. On to other announcements or programs or music. In the larger scheme of things, it is given the same priority as the rest of the gospel message. The leaders add it because everyone knows it is necessary, but they just don't realize *how* necessary it is.

In John 6:53–58, Jesus told those that followed him that he was the bread of life and that you must eat of his flesh and drink his blood. Otherwise, you were not included in his body. This was certainly a symbolic notion, pointing toward the act of communion. It was also meant to scandalize the Jews who listened intently to him, many of whom followed him around for the free food and drink. Immediately they assumed that he was literally instituting cannibalism. And in John 6:66, they left.

Communion was meant for you as a physical reminder that you were grafted into him and he into you. When we take the elements, consuming his body and drinking his blood, we *are* him, and he *is* us. At the Last Supper, when the disciples were gathered, Jesus took the bread and blessed it. Then he took wine and blessed it. This act included them in his suffering and ultimately in his death, burial, resurrection, *and* ascension to our Father's right hand.

You see? You are so much more valuable than you realize. Approach communion with a new mind set. It is not simply a symbol. It is the ultimate act of inclusion in him! You are *in* Jesus as he is in Father, and the fullness of the Godhead is *in* you.

11. JESUS, OUR FACE TO FACE

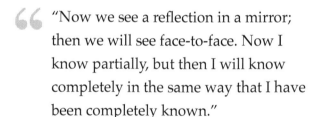 "Now we see a reflection in a mirror; then we will see face-to-face. Now I know partially, but then I will know completely in the same way that I have been completely known."

(1 Corinthians 13:12, CEB)

You hear a lot of people proclaiming to know mysteries, to know deep secrets or how God views things. The truth is that no one really knows anything. We are all looking in a darkened glass because our understanding is veiled by centuries, by millennia of misunderstandings. Some were intentional because certain men desired power to control the masses; most were unintentional because as men and women, we crave knowledge, and we supposedly think logically.

In this process of thinking logically, we forget to think through the filter of the love of Jesus and to see through his eyes. It's easy to put on our knowledge cap when we are faced with certain situations or trials and not show the heart of Jesus.

Then you will see that you are seated in him, in Jesus in heavenly places, blissfully looking into Father's eyes. You will begin to see him in everyone you experience, and you will love them as Jesus actively loves you. When you realize he is our face to face, then you will forever face his glory.

12. JESUS, OUR VICTORY

> "This decaying body must put on the undecaying one; this dying body must put on deathlessness. When the decaying puts on the undecaying, and the dying puts on the undying, then the saying that has been written will come true: Death is swallowed up in victory! Death, where's your victory gone? Death, where's your sting gone? The 'sting' of death is sin, and the power of sin is the law. But thank God! He gives us the victory, through our Lord Jesus the Messiah. So, my dear family, be firmly fixed, unshakeable, always full to overflowing with the

> Lord's work. In the Lord, as you know,
> the work you're doing will not be
> worthless."

(1 Corinthians 15:53–58, NTE)

Remember when you prayed for victory over that battle of addiction, disease, or situation? It felt like no answer was coming even though you tried to believe with all your might and strength. That desperate cry for overcoming the trial was exhausting and filled you with anxiety. You pushed harder and harder, but nothing happened.

While there are certainly some exceptions to this, for the most part, I have seen this time and time again, not only in my own life, but in the lives of others I have ministered to.

With all that said, you already have victory in Christ. You have already conquered the circumstance, the trial, the tribulation. All your enemies have been placed under your feet. Otherwise, you wouldn't be seated in Christ in heavenly places at the right hand of Father.

But you are.

You *are* seated in heavenly places in Jesus.

You don't have to strive or fight for your victory. The battle has already been won, and you didn't have to lift a finger.

13. JESUS, OUR REFUGE

 "God, you're such a safe and powerful place to find refuge! You're a proven help in time of trouble— more than enough and always available whenever I need you. So we will never fear even if every structure of support were to crumble away. We will not fear even when the earth quakes and shakes, moving mountains and casting them into the sea For the raging roar of stormy winds and crashing waves cannot erode our faith in you."

(Psalm 46:1–3, TPT)

Have you ever been afraid or hurt, and you ran into your room and shut the door? You felt safe even though only a two-inch–thick door stood between you and the challenge. You know what a hard time looks like: the anxiety and fear and uncertainty.

Before Jesus, that was the entire world. There was no escape, and the only answer was to take refuge in bushes and behind trees. Sin came in like a flood, and everyone fell to its desire. As a result, we hid from God.

Jesus came.

When he took his final breath on the cross, the veil was torn from top to bottom, ripped in half. This symbolized the fact that there was no need to hide anymore. If we needed to, we could take refuge in him. God was saying, "I am open to you; now open up to me."

In everything, remember God is your refuge and your strength. He is your victory and your banner. (See Exodus 17:15.)

14. JESUS, OUR STRENGTH

 "Comfort, comfort my people! says your God. But those who hope in the Lord will renew their strength; they will fly up on wings like eagles; they will run and not be tired; they will walk and not be weary."

(Isaiah 40:1, 31, CEB)

Most of us default to the first instinct of calling on the Lord when things don't seem to be going our way. We plead for strength in our weakness, healing in our sickness, life in our death. Truthfully, though, these responses are a result of our lack of knowledge about who we are.

Jesus truly became your strength and faced every challenge you would. He opened his arms to hold you tight during your despair and covered you with his massive wings when you were cold.

In the physical realm we live in, we face trouble and evil, people starving, freezing to death, and much more. All of these exist because humanity has been taught incorrectly, and those who perpetrate evil are operating from a lack of knowledge about who we are in the created works of God.

When we realize who we are, we produce good fruit. When we are in our ignorant state of mind, we produce rot.

With this said, when you are in Jesus, he becomes your strength. You actually become supermen and superwomen because he exchanged his strength for your weakness.

Jesus is your strength in times of weakness. He is even your strength in times of strength. He is your all in all.

15. JESUS, MY IDENTITY

 "Christ's resurrection is your resurrection too. This is why we are to yearn for all that is above, for that's where Christ sits enthroned at the place of all power, honor, and authority! Yes, feast on all the treasures of the heavenly realm and fill your thoughts with heavenly realities, and not with the distractions of the natural realm. Your crucifixion with Christ has severed the tie to this life, and now your true life is hidden away in God in Christ. And as Christ himself is seen for who he really is, who you really are will also be

> revealed, for you are now one with him in his glory!"
>
> (Colossians 3:1–4, TPT)

We have been taught about identity since our childhood. Magazines depicted humanity as aesthetically pleasing as possible, and TV shows flaunt almost perfect-looking actors and actresses. With the purest of motives, you were told as a child that you could be anything you wanted to be when you grew up. But when you didn't become what you wanted, your sense of identity seemed to disintegrate.

What if your identity was nothing like what you thought?

What if you were *more* than you could even imagine?

The truth is, your identity is so much more than your looks, your career, how you sound, or whatever else you hide in.

Speaking of hiding, as a child, you were taught all about the Garden of Eden—where Adam and Eve lived and worked as they stayed away from the Tree of the Knowledge of Good and Evil. We were taught that our identity was fallen because Adam ate from the very tree they were told to avoid. We were told that we were evil and that our best efforts were filthy rags. All of these were true at one point. Evil did enter through Adam, and that evil was known as sin. Sin affected all men. And in Adam, all men and women fell.

But when Jesus was born, he came with a mission to restore, reconcile, fulfill, and unite. In his death, burial, and resurrection, he exchanged his righteousness for our filthy rags, once for all.

Your identity is not found in the Tree of the Knowledge of Good and Evil.

No.

Your identity is *found* in Christ.

16. JESUS, MY FAITH

 "So then let's also run the race that is laid out in front of us, since we have such a great cloud of witnesses surrounding us. Let's throw off any extra baggage, get rid of the sin that trips us up, and fix our eyes on Jesus, faith's pioneer and perfecter. He endured the cross, ignoring the shame, for the sake of the joy that was laid out in front of him, and sat down at the right side of God's throne."

(Hebrews 12:1–2, CEB)

We are wrongly taught that we have to muster up faith to believe this mighty work of the cross, of Jesus Christ—that somehow when things don't happen, it's our fault. I personally lived in fear for years that my faith wasn't great enough, my belief not strong enough.

We hear stories about the mustard seed of faith (Luke 17:6) that Jesus insists is all we need to move the mountain from here to there, but I know I have stood at a mountain both spiritually and figuratively and neither moved. I was exercising faith so hard that sweat was pouring from my body and nothing. I know I am not alone in this, but this thinking was brought on because we were raised in incorrect theology and dogma.

Ephesians 2:8–9 talks about how we are saved through faith, and it isn't of ourselves but a gift. Jesus is our faith. He was the mustard seed buried in the earth that erupted from the grave as a new creation and you with him. He moved a mountain of rock to be with us in union; he ascended to Father and took us with him.

He is your faith in those challenging moments, holding you up even when you feel like falling. He is your faith when you mourn, in your tears, and in your strength. He is your faith even when you don't believe. Nothing can separate you from God's faith in you. (See Romans 8:28–38.) Not even you. Nothing you can do will make him forsake you.

17. JESUS, MY GOODNESS

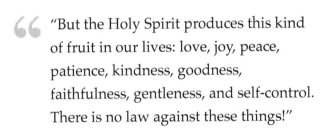 "But the Holy Spirit produces this kind of fruit in our lives: love, joy, peace, patience, kindness, goodness, faithfulness, gentleness, and self-control. There is no law against these things!"

(Galatians 5:22–23, NLT)

As I've said before, you have probably been taught for years that there is nothing good in you. That is to say, your flesh, your mind, your will, and your emotions are tainted by the fall of Adam. You are told that in order to be clean, you have to repeatedly wash in the waters of repentance and in the blood of Christ.

This is true to an extent—a very small extent. You see, you have been crucified with Christ, and you no longer live (Galatians 2:20). But you aren't dead; you are not a decaying mass of flesh with no hope. No, you did not face decay as Jesus didn't face it (Acts 2:27, Psalm 16:10). You were resurrected with Jesus to newness of life, his life (Romans 6:3–5). And now you are seated in heavenly places in Christ Jesus at the right hand of Father (Ephesians 2:6). Everything that is good in you is Jesus. He *is* your love, your joy, your peace, your patience, your kindness, your goodness, your faithfulness, your gentleness, and your self-control. No law stands against that; no law stands against you.

Deuteronomy 28:13 (paraphrase) states that the Lord will make you the head and not the tail; you will always be on top and never on the bottom. Of course, if read in context, it says, "If you keep My commands." If we keep Jesus and his goodness in us at our forefront, we fulfill everything in the law and commands because Jesus did.

You are the fulfillment of everything God desired for you even if you haven't realized it yet.

18. JESUS, OUR DWELLING PLACE

> "Lord, You have been our dwelling place in all generations."
>
> (Psalm 90:1, NASB)

> "Before the mountains were born, before you birthed the earth and the inhabited world—from forever in the past to forever in the future, you are God."
>
> (Psalm 90:2, CEB)

What does it mean to dwell or to have a place to

dwell? You might think of home unless your home life wasn't the greatest, in which case you might think of a place of comfort or relaxation.

When I think of home, I think about an especially hot day while I lay on mom's couch, relaxing in the air-conditioned house. The only noise I hear is the relaxing hum of the fan while I sleep.

In all generations—past to present—God has been our dwelling place. You are not excluded but included in him. In him, you can snuggle up on the most comfortable couch, enjoy the warmth of a toasty fire, or be refreshed by the coolest breeze.

In him, there is no striving, only rest. In that rest, there is joy. In that joy, there is peace. You see, you are so important to the God of all the universe. You are not disposable; you are not replaceable. His joy in you is not fulfilled until you have joy in him.

He will always leave the cliques, the groups, the ones who have it altogether for you. Then he will rejoice and bring you back to his home on his shoulders, where there is much celebration at your unity with him.

He is that place of comfort, relaxation, and rest. He will always be your dwelling place.

19. JESUS, MY LIGHT

> "Jesus said, 'You're asking the wrong question. You're looking for someone to blame. There is no such cause-effect here. Look instead for what God can do. We need to be energetically at work for the One who sent me here, working while the sun shines. When night falls, the workday is over. For as long as I am in the world, there is plenty of light. I am the world's Light.'"
>
> (John 9:3–5, MSG)

God dwells in an unapproachable light (1 Timothy 6:16).

That light is you.

But you aren't lit by anything outside of Jesus. You are a torch, waiting for the breath of God to ignite a flame in you. God wouldn't send Jesus, the master flame, to ignite you and then hide you (Luke 11:33). He instead wants to put you on a hill so that you shine for miles. He wants to make you a bright and shining star in the darkness, not a grain of sand trampled underfoot.

This is not due to anything you have done because you can't do anything to earn it. You just are. Just like God *is* love, you just *are* in his love and light and celebration.

For example, you can make the following analogy about light. If you shine a bright light at a brick wall, any flaws or imperfections can be spotted on the other side of the wall. The light shining through one little crack or hole can brighten an otherwise dark room. As Jesus said, "You are the light of the world." (See Matthew 5:14–16.) And Jesus is that light within us.

Shine like the bright star you are, and you'll suddenly attract others into your orbit that you can love on more deeply like Jesus loved you.

20. JESUS, OUR LOVER

> "For you reach into my heart. With one flash of your eyes I am undone by your love, my beloved, my equal, my bride. You leave me breathless—I am overcome by merely a glance from your worshiping eyes, for you have stolen my heart. I am held hostage by your love and by the graces of righteousness shining upon you. How satisfying to me, my equal, my bride. Your love is my finest wine—intoxicating and thrilling. And your sweet, perfumed praises—so exotic, so pleasing. Your loving words are like the honeycomb to me; your tongue releases milk and honey, for I find

the Promised Land flowing within you. The fragrance of your worshiping love surrounds you with scented robes of white. My darling bride, my private paradise, fastened to my heart. A secret spring are you that no one else can have — my bubbling fountain hidden from public view. What a perfect partner to me now that I have you."

(Song of Songs 4:9–12, TPT)

Do you remember the first time you fell in love? How the person's presence, voice, their scent, and even just the mere thought of their name made you quiver with excitement?

That first love is something that most of us have experienced whether directly or from afar. You might have had a crush that you thought was love. Maybe you even had a teenage relationship that you thought would last forever.

The heartbreak that ensued afterward was bitter, and many tears followed. You might have flared with anger against the person you were once obsessed with.

Imagine God's potent love for his creation in the Garden. Everywhere you looked, life sprang forth. God was so in love with Adam and Eve that he wanted to protect them from anything that could harm them, so he told them to avoid this great big fruit-bearing tree in the Garden. They did. At least for a while.

But then the serpent came and began to whisper into Eve's ear. It probably said something like, "God will love you more if you eat this fruit." Or "You will be smarter and more beautiful if you consume this fruit."

Imagine that conversation, using any wording you like. It probably involved the serpent trying to cause doubt to creep into Eve's mind. She fell for it and consumed the fruit.

You know the rest of the story. She convinced Adam; he ate; we fell. Sin entered the world through one act of disobedience, which set God's plan of reconciliation into motion.

He sent his Son to become the fruit we would eat from instead of the Tree of the Knowledge of Good and Evil. He revealed his timeless love through the ages through Jesus, and Jesus revealed God to us like only Adam and Eve might have known before.

Through one act of obedience, sin was destroyed —for all men, once for all. Jesus was resurrected and ascended to the right hand of Father. He is not only sitting but dancing and singing the most epic love ballad of all time over us.

You are the treasure in the field that he sold everything to obtain; you are the pearl of great price that he sold everything to have. (See Matthew 13:44–46.) You are the love that he died for, that he gave it all for so that he could hold you in his arms.

21. YOU ARE HIS TREASURE

 "The kingdom of heaven is like a treasure that somebody hid in a field, which someone else found and covered up. Full of joy, the finder sold everything and bought that field."

(Matthew 13:44, CEB)

The idea that Jesus is the treasure in the field and that you must sell everything to obtain him has been preached for a couple thousand years. With few exceptions, this coincides with much of the doctrine in the church today. I know I was taught this growing up.

I felt like I had to earn Jesus (and my salvation). I was convinced that I had to give up everything that brought me joy to obtain him. Somehow I had to do something to gain this treasure. I didn't know how I would do it, but I had to obtain this treasure.

Then my eyes were opened. I saw myself buried in the field, and Jesus selling everything he had for me. His desire for me was so potent that when he obtained the field, he breathlessly dug me out of the miry clay and held me close to his chest. I could feel his heartbeat synchronizing with mine.

I tell you this story in hopes that you can put yourself in that position and realize how important you are. How cherished you are. How much Jesus treasures you.

God didn't hide you in that field; the years and years of teaching that you were dirty, separated from him, did that. He had to find you; when he did, he took the stripes that you thought God was waiting to give you. He died the death that you were told you deserved. He was buried in the dirt and tomb reserved for you. Then he broke forth and rose from the miry clay as a representation of God finding you.

You see, God sold everything to obtain you, gave

everything to get you, and drained every ounce of blood to purify you. He gave everything of himself to get you, to bring you into unity with him.

22. JESUS, OUR WHISPER

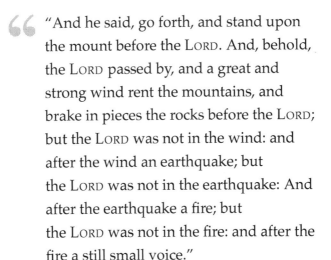
"And he said, go forth, and stand upon the mount before the Lord. And, behold, the Lord passed by, and a great and strong wind rent the mountains, and brake in pieces the rocks before the Lord; but the Lord was not in the wind: and after the wind an earthquake; but the Lord was not in the earthquake: And after the earthquake a fire; but the Lord was not in the fire: and after the fire a still small voice."

(1 Kings 19:11–12, KJV)

Through the Trinity, God has been in a constant union forever, forehead to forehead, eye to eye, speaking to each other for eternity. In their communion, galaxies were formed, stars, the Earth. Their greatest creation is you, and God wasn't about to lose you.

We might have lost his voice for a time, but that doesn't mean he stopped speaking. He has continuously spoken over you for your future and follows close behind to protect you from your past (Psalm 139). He leans into you and places his forehead upon yours: he doesn't need to yell.

I heard this story from a friend on Facebook. A coworker of hers is normally loud and very obnoxious. But one day, the coworker asked if she could do my friend's makeup, to which she agreed.

This normally loud coworker taught her a lesson, and the retelling of the story taught me one as well. The woman leaned in and began to whisper about what she was doing. My friend was amazed at how quiet she was and made a remark to that effect. The woman smiled and said that when you are face to face, you only need to whisper.

You see, Jesus is face to face with you, his eyes peering deeply into yours. He speaks in a still small voice, but because he is so close, he doesn't have to shout to get your attention.

23. JESUS, OUR UNDERSTANDING

 "Be glad in the Lord always! Again I say, be glad! Let your gentleness show in your treatment of all people. The Lord is near. Don't be anxious about anything; rather, bring up all of your requests to God in your prayers and petitions, along with giving thanks. Then the peace of God that exceeds all understanding will keep your hearts and minds safe in Christ Jesus."

(Philippians 4:4–7, CEB)

For centuries, man has tried to define who Jesus was and is. The only problem with this is that discovering Jesus has been more of an academic experience rather than one of abiding. We attempt to understand who Jesus is through knowledge, writings, and historical accounts. But you can only learn so much from this type of study.

Have you ever just sat in the quiet, eyes closed and mind focused on Jesus? I believe you will learn more from one-on-one time than you ever will through academic study. It is impossible to learn the heart of something through the mind.

We can think we get it, but that still small voice of Holy Spirit truly teaches us. Like Mary, who sat at the feet of Jesus, we must rest to fully understand the motivations of God, and even then, we can only partially grasp it. (See Luke 10:38–42.)

Our understanding of God is completely wrapped up in Jesus. He is the fullness of deity in bodily form. And he rests in you.

24. YOU ARE HIS MASTERPIECE

> "Salvation is not a reward for the good things we have done, so none of us can boast about it. For we are God's masterpiece. He has created us anew in Christ Jesus, so we can do the good things he planned for us long ago."
>
> (Ephesians 2:9–10, NLT)

You are a masterpiece, not a throwaway piece. You are beautiful, lovely, desirable to the Lord. Not because of what you have done, but because of what Jesus has done. Not because of what you haven't done, but because of Jesus. He looks through the exterior, no matter how rough, and finds that diamond deep within. He makes his house near that diamond.

The darkness you once had has been abolished by the light (John 3:19), and now you are a city on a hill, lit up so that everyone can see you. (See Matthew 5:14.) You might not be what you think you should be, but Jesus sees you as complete in him. Your completeness is not tied to what you do, just like a canvas cannot force paint strokes without the aid of the artist. Your place in him has nothing to do with works but everything to do with his faith in you.

He created the heavens and the stars, the moon and the sun, all of creation. Yet he still held you up beside all of this and called you his greatest creation, his *masterpiece*!

25. JESUS, MY PROVIDER

> "Ask, and it shall be given you; seek, and ye shall find; knock, and it shall be opened unto you: For every one that asks receives; and he that seeks finds; and to him that knocks it shall be opened. Or what man is there of you, whom if his son ask bread, will he give him a stone? Or if he asks for a fish, will he give him a serpent? If ye then, being evil, know how to give good gifts unto your children, how much more shall your Father which is in heaven give good things to them that ask him?"

(Matthew 7:7–11, KJV, slight paraphrase)

I have been exposed to many great men of God in my life. One of them once told a story in a sermon on verse 7. He said that we should ask, seek, and knock. The acronym for ask, seek, and knock is simply A.S.K. I know it's a little kitschy, but it is also catchy. We have not because we ask not (James 4:2–3), and if we would simply ask for help in what we need to achieve, we would have it.

This is not a name-it-and-claim-it paradigm, even though this verse is often taken out of context to justify that theology. This is more about the attributes of our God as a provider. For centuries and millennia, man asked for deliverance from the hands of the evil one. Not that they were ever in the actual hands of the evil one because their captivity was mostly self-imposed. But because they constantly asked, he sent Jesus, the lamb of the world.

We often ask for things, expecting one result but getting an entirely different outcome. They begged for a Messiah, not a feeble carpenter. They demanded a warrior, a warrior to destroy Egypt, Babylon, Rome, and all their enemies. But they got a cunning, sarcastic, and witty guy from Galilee, the armpit of the world. They even had a saying that no good thing comes from Galilee. (See John 1:46.)

They demanded a sacrifice, so God gave them Jesus. They demanded a warrior, so God gave them the Lion of Judah. They demanded a King, so God gave them the King of all kings.

Jesus became the way to reach Father. He made the road flat and easy to travel because he walked the hard road on our behalf. He desires to give you all good things. But sometimes the good thing he gives you is not what you expect and might not be perceived as good when you receive it. Even so, what father would ever give his child a snake when the child asks for a fish?

Every good and perfect gift is from the Lord (James 1:17).

26. JESUS, OUR DRINK

> "Then Jesus said unto them, Verily, verily, I say unto you, Except ye eat the flesh of the Son of man, and drink his blood, ye have no life in you."
>
> (John 6:53, KJV)

It is so easy to fall into the old mindset and to drink from our own supply of the vineyard. We have moments where we retreat into ourselves and forsake others. We tend to trust ourselves, not others, but Jesus insists that he is the living river that never runs dry. Your own supply will run dry if you continue to drink of yourself; even the mud will turn into hard clay.

Remember the woman at the well. (See John 4.) Jesus engaged her on the premise that he was thirsty, only to reveal to her that she was actually the one who was thirsty. She was dry as a bone and operating from the mindset that she could supply her own needs. All the while, her inability to supply her own needs led to multiple husbands and love affairs.

When we retreat into ourselves, the first thing that often suffers is our relationship with God. Even though we have been led to a river, we turn away and see the dryness of where we came from, sometimes wanting to return to it because of how comfortable it was. The Hebrews wanted to return to bondage and slavery because they had a difficult path to follow to the Promised Land.

Jesus is your drink, the well that will never run dry, the river that will never stop flowing. He is the water that will never part ways with you because it is completely in your belly. Jesus and his kingdom are within you. *In you* the fullness of the Godhead dwells. *In you* dwells the completeness of who he Is. This is not a rosy message to tickle your ears as it is difficult to understand and even harder to practice. That is why we are called to rest, to abide in his vineyard, attached to his vine.

He will never run dry.
He will never run out.
He is your portion.
He is your supply.
Drink deep of his well!

27. JESUS, OUR SHOWBREAD

> "Set the bread of the presence on the table so it is always in front of me."
>
> (Exodus 25:30, CEB)

> "Jesus replied, "I am the bread of life. Whoever comes to me will never go hungry, and whoever believes in me will never be thirsty."
>
> (John 6:35, CEB)

You have heard that Jesus is the bread of life, but the

implications of that are more far-reaching than what one verse says. In the temple forged by human hands was a table, and upon that table sat a candle that stayed lit at all times. In front of that candle was a loaf of bread called the showbread, translated the bread of presence.

This bread never left that table, and once a week, it was refreshed with new bread. The old bread was taken to the temple priest who ate this bread while in the temple or holy place. This was a foreshadowing of communion; when the priests consumed this bread, they were actually entering the presence of God.

According to the Law of Moses, only priests (Levites) were allowed to partake of this bread and only in the holy place or temple.

Enter Jesus. In John 6, he makes the radical assertion that he is this bread that has never left the presence of God, and that in order to have life in you, you have to eat of this bread. The Jews understood that he was referring to the showbread and were scandalized. First, the temple was still standing. Second, the showbread was still sitting on the table in the temple in front of the ever-burning candle. Third, was Jesus actually saying that he was edible? That in order to have life, he would have to become bread so that they could eat him?

You can see why so many people left. They were fearful, disgusted, and felt that the time they had put into following this guy was wasted. To them, he was a lunatic, insane. Right after that, Jesus asked his disciples if they were going to leave too. The remainder of them responded emphatically that they had nowhere to go because he alone had the words of life.

Jesus is the bread of the presence, the showbread, and you are the holy place. He resides in you and operates through you. He is placed on the table in that holy place in the presence of the fire of Holy Spirit. You have been made holy through him, so you are united in him.

28: JESUS, OUR FAITH

> "Therefore, since we are surrounded by so great a cloud of witnesses, let us also lay aside every weight, and sin which clings so closely, and let us run with endurance the race that is set before us, looking to Jesus, the founder and perfecter of our faith, who for the joy that was set before him endured the cross, despising the shame, and is seated at the right hand of the throne of God."

(Hebrews 12:1–2, ESV)

You often feel as if you have to muster up the faith to do something. You feel that God put this glorious gift right in front of you that you cannot see or touch, and you just have to have enough faith to obtain it. You have to believe hard enough and strong enough. Yet that nagging voice in your head keeps saying that God won't come through. The harder you push, the louder it echoes.

It is easy to fall into that trap. But don't worry, the best news you have ever heard will set you free. This news would obviously be impossible to believe, so Jesus became your faith so that you didn't have to faith it on your own. Just rest at Father's right hand while he does amazing things through you for others, in you, and for you.

He endured the cross in the most epic love story ever told. He pushed you off the train tracks as the oncoming train barreled toward you, your destruction sure. He was hit in your place. That train is not Father; it was death, death that we rightfully deserved through the vast amounts of sin we had committed. But he took the collision on your behalf.

He took your stripes and punishment; he took your nails; he took your death, not as an example for us to follow, but as an example of us.

We can easily fall into the trap of religion and the massive amounts of empty requirements that religion feeds you. Be assured, sons and daughters of God, that is not for you and never was. You are a child of the Most High God, begotten in the flesh in Jesus. You are the light in which Father dwells, the stars reflect you.

The next time you feel pressured to muster up enough faith to believe, just be like Mary and sit at his feet. Let him faith it for you so that you don't have to fake it for him.

29. JESUS, THE DEFEAT OF OUR ENEMY

> "The thief comes only to steal and kill and destroy. I came that they may have life and have it abundantly."
>
> (John 10:10, ESV)

I was having a conversation the other day with a friend who kept lamenting about the enemy's continuous attacks against her. She believed this and was filled with tremendous anguish. I could see the fear in her eyes, and I heard Jesus speak.

"Peace, be still."

The enemy came as a thief in the night, hoping to

steal, kill, and destroy. But Jesus came so that we could have life and have it more abundantly. The enemy is completely under your feet because you are seated in heavenly places in Christ Jesus. The enemy is like an ant trampled underfoot with a megaphone, trying to convince you that he is bigger than he really is.

He has no power; he is destitute, trying to cling to an existence that was stripped from him because of his rebellion. His biggest desire is to distract you, to keep you from realizing who you are. You are sons and daughters of God, no matter what the enemy keeps trying to shout at you from his microscopic megaphone.

Jesus totally defeated everything on the cross: the enemy, death, sin, *everything*. You have been perfected in Christ, and in Christ you are perfect and shiny and clean. Every single blemish in you and on you has been thoroughly wiped away.

Take joy in this because the enemy has been defeated. All he has is his little megaphone, but you have the entire kingdom of God in your belly!

30. JESUS, THE SONG OF YOU

> "For you reach into my heart. With one flash of your eyes I am undone by your love, my beloved, my equal, my bride. You leave me breathless—I am overcome by merely a glance from your worshiping eyes, for you have stolen my heart. I am held hostage by your love and by the graces of righteousness shining upon you. How satisfying to me, my equal, my bride. Your love is my finest wine—intoxicating and thrilling. And your sweet, perfumed praises—so exotic, so pleasing."
>
> (Song of Songs 4:9–10, TPT)

Think of the corniest romantic comedy you have ever seen. Add to that even more of the rom-com tropes you have come to love (or hate) over the years. Bag it all up and that is how Jesus feels about you times infinity. During these last thirty days, we have unpacked what many believe is the gospel truth and instead revealed the true gospel, the gospel of His relentless, unceasing love for you.

This gospel tells how Jesus has taken you and cleaned you, how he has perfected you and reconciled you to our loving Father. This Father was never angry with you but was always madly in love with you. He was *so* in love that he took a piece of himself and allowed us to kill that part to reveal the lengths to which he would go so that you could have an intimate relationship with him.

Religion would have you believe that you somehow earn his love or that you are elected to receive his love while others perish. It would have you fearfully sharing this condemning and shame-filled message in hopes of saving those through the control it espouses.

Religion would put you on a course to do more, have less, and feel ashamed.

The gospel would have you free, living an abundant life that you otherwise could not have when you were trapped in the chains of a false identity. Your identity is Jesus, who fully indwells you and you in him. In you, resides the totality of the kingdom of God From your belly flows rivers upon rivers upon rivers of living water. When others drink from this river, they will no longer thirst for a life of depravity. And when you drink from it, you will be as satisfied in him as he is in you.

The gospel is the *Song of You*, a song written and composed before the foundations of the earth to win you from a life of death and sin into a life filled with light and his love.

CONTACT INFORMATION

You can reach James at his personal FB page here.
https://www.facebook.com/awarriorscry

This is his ministry page here.
https://www.facebook.com/thewarriorscry/

You can email James at thewarriorscry@gmail.com

ABOUT THE AUTHOR

James has walked with the Lord since 1996. He was indirectly saved through the Brownsville Revival after a speaker from the revival came to his church. During the summer of 2017, his theology radically changed after he encountered Jesus in a completely different way. He has hosted a podcast, "The Warrior's Cry," since 2016 and does Facebook live videos several times a week on his Facebook page. His ministry is also called "The Warrior's Cry," which centers on revealing our identities in Christ and bringing unity to a divided church.

You can usually find James enjoying the presence of Holy Spirit, worshipping in his car, or singing with the praise and worship team at New Covenant Church, in Clyde, NC. James resides with his wife Amber in the Great Smoky Mountains of North Carolina.

Made in the USA
Lexington, KY
27 December 2018